P9-DSZ-338

For

THAT SPECIAL

Mother

Loving Reflections

Edited by Phyllis D'Aprile Alston

Designed by Michel Design

PETER PAUPER PRESS, INC.
WHITE PLAINS · NEW YORK

*With love to my mother Rosemary, mother-in-law
Mary Rose, Grandma Campbell, Grandma D'Aprile,
sisters Kathy and Maureen, and Tiffanie and Dana*

*Thanks to Claudine Gandolfi for
assistance in compilation.*

Copyright © 1995, 1996
Peter Pauper Press, Inc.
202 Mamaroneck Avenue
White Plains, NY 10601
All rights reserved
ISBN 0-88088-870-9
Printed in Singapore
7 6 5 4 3 2

Introduction

*F*rom the minute we are born our closest relationship is with our mother. *That Special Mother* examines the special bond between mother and child. Each quotation brings out some form of mother wisdom, wit, or feeling.

As that wise Jewish proverb states: *God could not be everywhere, and therefore he made mothers*. Mothers abound in this Keepsake, which is filled with the experiences of dozens of mothers, children, and those who have witnessed the tie between the two.

We hope that you will treasure this book almost as much as you would cherish a child, and believe that you will enjoy its wisdom for many years to come. As a gift, it is a way of saying "thank you" or "I love you" to a very special person.

ABOUT MOTHERS

*A*ll that I am my mother made me.

JOHN QUINCY ADAMS

*J*ust as breast milk cannot be duplicated, neither can a mother.

SALLY E. SHAYWITZ

*M*y mother was a wit, but never a sentimental one. Once, when somebody in our house stepped on our cat's paw, she turned to the cat and said sternly, "I told you not to go around barefoot!"

ZERO MOSTEL

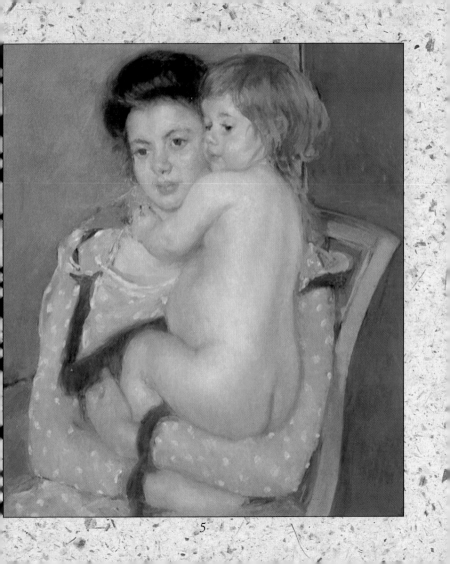

If you would reform the world from its errors and vices, begin by enlisting the mothers.

CHARLES SIMMONS

The role of mother is probably the most important career a woman can have.

JANET MARY RILEY

My mom was the most fantastic woman in the world. She only went to the fifth grade, but she knew there was nothing wrong with my brain. I just couldn't see.

RAY CHARLES

Mothers of the race [are] the most important actors in the grand drama of human progress.

ELIZABETH CADY STANTON

Biology is the least of what makes someone a mother.

OPRAH WINFREY

A mother's love endures through all; in good repute, in bad repute, in the face of the world's condemnation, a mother still loves on.

WASHINGTON IRVING

*N*o joy in nature is so sublimely affecting as the joy of a mother at the good fortune of her child.

JEAN PAUL RICHTER

*S*ome are kissing mothers and some are scolding mothers, but it is love just the same, and most mothers kiss and scold together.

PEARL S. BUCK

The only mothers it is safe to forget on Mother's Day are the good ones.

MIGNON MCLAUGHLIN

My mother used to say, "He who angers you, conquers you!" But my mother was a saint.

ELIZABETH KENNY

A mother never realizes that her children are no longer children.

HOLBROOK JACKSON

You may have seen my mother Sarah in my music.

QUINCY JONES

*S*he did not understand how her father could have reached such age and such eminence without learning that all mothers are as infallible as any pope and more righteous than any saint.

FRANCES NEWMAN

*M*others are the lives which move education.

FRANCES E. W. HARPER

*B*eing a housewife and a mother is the biggest job in the world, but if it doesn't interest you, don't do it. . . . I would have made a terrible mother.

KATHARINE HEPBURN

*C*hrissie's the best mom. To see her love for this child at all hours of the day and night, to see how she holds him and cares for him and kisses him and loves him. It's just incredible.

ANDY MILL,
HUSBAND OF CHRIS EVERT

$\mathcal{M}$y mother never gave up on me. I messed up in school so much they were sending me home, but my mother sent me right back.

DENZEL WASHINGTON

$\mathcal{T}$he ultimate revenge on this liberal mom who didn't care what her kid looked like is that he's a looker. He is beautiful.

JANE WALLACE

$\mathcal{I}$t is generally admitted, and very frequently proved, that virtue and genius, and all the natural good qualities which men possess, are derived from their mothers.

HOOK

$\mathcal{W}$ho ran to help me when I fell,
And would some pretty story tell,
Or kiss the place to make it well?
    My mother.

ANN TAYLOR

*T*he good mother says not, Will you? but gives.

GEORGE HERBERT

I am most proud of how she's raised Chelsea. . . . [She was able to be] a wonderfully successful person as a good mother and wife, and grow over the years . . .

BILL CLINTON,
ABOUT HILLARY

*T*hink carefully about having that baby. Not to have it would be a great loss. To have it too late greatly increases the health hazards for you and the child. To have it without a commitment to it would be a great tragedy.

BEVERLY SILLS

$\mathcal{D}$ad taught me self-respect. Everything else I learned from Mom, including how to make a chocolate cake.

DAVID FARENTINO

$\mathcal{M}$y mother told me not to learn anything that I didn't want to do, so I never learned to wash a floor or clean a toilet.

SHARI LEWIS

$\mathcal{M}$y mother did just fine raising three of us by herself.

TEVIN CAMPBELL

$\mathcal{M}$y mother realized she was dying and would not have the chance to give me as much as she would have liked before she departed. So she crammed as much into me as she possibly could in those fourteen years. I didn't know exactly what she was doing at the time, but years later I realized how that care and love, the moral support sustained me.

GORDON PARKS

*M*otherhood [has made me] calmer, happier, more tolerant.

SUSAN RUTTAN

*E*ven today, when I think about my mother for any reason, what first jumps to mind are memories of her telling me that she loved me more than anyone else in the world.

BILL RUSSELL

*W*ho is best taught? He who has first learned from his mother.

TALMUD

14

*T*he mother-child relationship is paradoxical and, in a sense, tragic. It requires the most intense love on the mother's side, yet this very love must help the child grow away from the mother and to become fully independent.

ERICH FROMM

*M*ore than in any other human relationship, overwhelmingly more, motherhood means being instantly interruptible, responsive, responsible.

TILLIE OLSEN

*I*f a mother is forced to cut too many corners, she may find herself going around in circles.

MARCELENE COX

*W*e bear the world, and we make it. . . . There was never a great man who had not a great mother—it is hardly an exaggeration.

OLIVE SCHREINER

*C*hildren are the anchors that hold a mother to life.

SOPHOCLES

*T*o describe my mother would be to write about a hurricane in its perfect power.

MAYA ANGELOU

*T*he very essence of motherly love is to care for the child's growth, and that means to want the child's separation from herself.

ERICH FROMM

*T*he commonest fallacy among women is that simply having children makes one a mother—which is as absurd as believing that having a piano makes one a musician.

SYDNEY J. HARRIS

*O*nly mothers can think of the future—because they give birth to it in their children.

MAXIM GORKY

*T*he only thing that seems eternal and natural in motherhood is ambivalence.

JANE LAZARRE

*M*otherhood affords an instant identity. First, through wifehood, you are somebody's wife; then you are somebody's mother. Both give not only identity and activity, but status and stardom of a kind.

BETTY ROLLIN

*A*nd it came to me, and I knew what I had to have before my soul would rest. I wanted to belong—to belong to my mother. And in return—I wanted my mother to belong to me.

GLORIA VANDERBILT

*T*here is no slave out of heaven like a loving woman; and, of all loving women, there is no such slave as a mother.

HENRY WARD BEECHER

I hope they are still making women like my Momma. She always told me to do the right thing, to have pride in myself and that a good name is better than money.

JOE LOUIS

A mother is not a person to lean on, but a person to make leaning unnecessary.

DOROTHY CANFIELD FISHER

*H*ousewives and mothers seldom find it practicable to come out on strike. They have no union, anyway.

ELAINE MORGAN

*T*he human woman gives birth just as the earth gives birth to the plants. She gives nourishment, as the plants do. So woman magic and earth magic are the same. They are related. And the personification of the energy that gives birth to forms and nourishes forms is properly female.

JOSEPH CAMPBELL

*M*other is the name for God in the lips and hearts of children.

WILLIAM MAKEPEACE THACKERAY

*I*t is odd how all men develop the notion, as they grow older, that their mothers were wonderful cooks. I have yet to meet a man who will admit that his mother was a kitchen assassin, and nearly poisoned him.

ROBERTSON DAVIES

*E*ven if your mother is not a good woman, she is your mother, nevertheless.

AFRICAN PROVERB

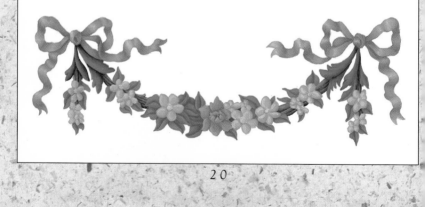

$\mathcal{Q}$: What's the greatest joy of motherhood?
A: Watching your kids grow and knowing that, whether they become president of the United States or just the ringleader of some bizarre religious cult, you helped make it happen.

MARGE SIMPSON

"$\mathcal{Y}$oung mother."—And so you think a baby is a thing of beauty and a joy forever? Well, the idea is pleasing, but not original; every cow thinks the same of its own calf.

MARK TWAIN

$\mathcal{S}$pock, shlock, don't talk to me about that stuff. A man doesn't know how to bring up children until he's been a mother.

DAN GREENBURG

$\mathcal{M}$other was the absolutely dominating force in all our lives. Even her mere existence in these last years was a sort of centre around which we revolved, in thought if not in our actual movements. We shall be living henceforth in an essentially different world.

GEORGE SANTAYANA

$\mathcal{E}$very beetle is a gazelle in the eyes of its mother.

MOORISH PROVERB

$\mathcal{T}$here are only two lasting bequests we can hope to give our children. One of these is roots; the other wings.

HODDING CARTER

$\mathcal{M}$y father was poor. . . . He thought that with the music there was very little to do, and he thought better to be a carpenter. He was thinking seriously of that for me, but my mother said to him, "This boy has a gift, and it is our duty to follow it." She was a wonderful woman.

PABLO CASALS

It's clear that most American children suffer too much mother and too little father.

GLORIA STEINEM

The mother is a matchless beast.

JAMES KELLY

Some mothers need happy children; others need unhappy ones—otherwise they cannot prove their maternal virtues.

FRIEDRICH W. NIETZSCHE

I regard no man as poor who has a godly mother.

ABRAHAM LINCOLN

*B*lessed are the mothers of the earth. They combine the practical and spiritual into the workable way of human life.

WILLIAM L. STINGER

*E*very mother is like Moses. She does not enter the promised land. She prepares a world she will not see.

POPE PAUL VI

A printed card means nothing except that you are too lazy to write to the woman who has done more for you than anyone in the world. And candy! You take a box to Mother—and then eat most of it yourself. A pretty sentiment.

ANNA JARVIS,
FOUNDER OF MOTHER'S DAY

*I*f there were no schools to take the children away from home part of the time, the insane asylum would be filled with mothers.

EDGAR WATSON HOWE

*N*ature records the male but a secondary and comparatively humble place in the home, the breeding-place of the race; he may compensate himself if he will, by seeking adventure or renown in the world outside. The mother is the child's supreme parent.

HAVELOCK ELLIS

A suburban mother's role is to deliver children obstetrically once, and by car forever after.

PETER DE VRIES

A mother's love is indeed the golden link that binds youth to age; and he is still but a child, however time may have furrowed his cheek, or silvered his brow, who can yet recall, with a softened heart, the fond devotion, or the gentle chidings, of the best friend that God ever gives us.

CHRISTIAN NESTELL BOVEE

*E*ven a secret agent can't lie to a Jewish mother.

PETER MALKIN

$\mathscr{T}$o me, my mother is the most incredibly beautiful woman in the world. . . . I remember my mother saying, ". . . There's always going to be someone more beautiful than you, always someone smarter than you, always someone more talented than you. So instead of working to try to beat everyone, just do your own thing."

ZOE CASSAVETES,
DAUGHTER OF GENA ROWLANDS

When I was little I wasn't aware that I had these, like, beautiful people as parents. I thought my mom's whole purpose was to be my mom. That's how she made me feel. . . . She always wanted my sister and me to look like we just walked out of Pierre Deux. Very French little dresses. I was a little ballerina, like a little princess. I loved it. I loved my childhood. And I loved my mom.

NATASHA GREGSON WAGNER,
DAUGHTER OF NATALIE WOOD

My mother wanted me to be her wings, to fly as she never quite had the courage to do.

ERICA JONG

In my generation, many of us knew that we did not want to be like our mothers, even when we loved them. We could not help but see their disappointment. . . . Strangely, many mothers who loved their daughters—and mine was one—did not want their daughters to grow up like them either. They knew we needed something more.

BETTY FRIEDAN

Everybody's mother still cares.

LILLIAN HELLMAN

A mother is a mother, ye Zulus!

AFRICAN PROVERB

You know where I get my fighting spirit? It all started with my mother.

BILL CLINTON

$\mathcal{T}$he only thing that brings a mother undiluted satisfaction is her relation to a son. It is quite the almost complete relationship between human beings, and the one that is the most free from ambivalence.

SIGMUND FREUD

$\mathcal{Y}$ou can choose your friends, but you only have one mother.

MAX SHULMAN

$\mathcal{N}$ever say anything on the phone that you wouldn't want your mother to hear at your trial.

SYDNEY BIDDLE BARROWS

$\mathcal{G}$od could not be everywhere, and therefore he made mothers.

JEWISH PROVERB

$\mathcal{A}$ll that I am, or hope to be, I owe to my angel mother.

ABRAHAM LINCOLN

As she supplies the affection and care that make a contented home, each mother is strengthening the individuals within her own circle as well as in the nation.

EARL E. CHANLEY

Erotic love begins with separateness, and ends in oneness. Motherly love begins with oneness, and leads to separateness.

ERICH FROMM

You've always been there for me, sharing in my pains and in my joys, helping me in every way possible and never asking for anything in return. You're the best friend I've ever had.

KIMBERLIN BROWN,
TO HER MOTHER

33

My mother told me stories all the time, . . . And in all of those stories she told me who I was, who I was supposed to be, whom I came from, and who would follow me. In this way, she taught me the meaning of the words she said, that all life is a circle and everything has a place within it. That's what she said and what she showed me in the things she did and the way she lives.

PAULA GUNN ALLEN

It is not that I half knew my mother. I knew half of her: the lower half—her lap, legs, feet, her hands and wrists as she bent forward.

FLANN O'BRIEN

$\mathcal{O}$f all the rights of women, the greatest is to be a mother.

LIN YUTANG

$\mathcal{M}$other's personality enriched our lives beyond measure. . . . Mother's varied talents combined with Dad's perception and storytelling skill to produce an environment in which love and creative imagination prevailed over adversity.

JEAN AND KATHY GODFREY

$\mathcal{W}$ho sat and watched my infant head
When sleeping in my cradle bed,
And tears of sweet affection shed?
      My mother.

ANN TAYLOR

$\mathcal{W}$hen my mother had to get dinner for eight she'd just make enough for sixteen and only serve half.

GRACIE ALLEN

*H*e that would the daughter win,
Must with the mother first begin.

JOHN RAY

*M*y mother taught me underneath a tree,
And sitting down before the heat of day,
She took me on her lap and kissèd me,
And pointing to the east, began to say:

Look on the rising sun: there God does live,
And gives his light, and gives his heat away;
And flowers and trees and beasts and men receive
Comfort in morning, joy in the noon day. . . . "

WILLIAM BLAKE,
THE LITTLE BLACK BOY

*W*hen I think of my mother, I think of someone who is very eccentric. . . . She puts a lot of warmth and energy into things; she never does anything halfway.

STEPHANIE AGNEW

*N*o one but doctors and mothers know what it means to have interruptions.

KARL A. MENNINGER

*M*y mother would go out in a rowboat with a bunch of books and she would drop anchor and read to us. She would often read what she wanted to read and I suppose it was a way of getting her reading time in. But I think she genuinely enjoyed spending this time with us and I realized later just how amazing it was.

NANCY WILLARD

*N*ow, as always, the most automated appliance in a household is the mother.

BEVERLY JONES

I saw her working, being the emotional and spiritual leader in our family. She had almost a fanatical emphasis on education. We got encyclopedias, and she struggled to make those payments. She kept saying, "I don't care what you do, but be the best at it."

JUDGE SONIA SOTOMAYOR

*M*ost of all the other beautiful things in life come by twos and threes, by dozens and hundreds. Plenty of roses, stars, sunsets, rainbows, brothers and sisters, aunts and cousins, but only one mother in the whole world.

KATE DOUGLAS WIGGIN

*M*y mother was an inspiration to me, teaching me that there was something to be had in every experience in life, even in dying.

JAMES KIBERD

*M*y mother is a woman who speaks with her life as much as with her tongue.

KESAYA E. NODA

$\mathcal{I}$ think Mom and I are a lot alike and that's because I've tried to be like her. I thank her for teaching me good values, good morals, good discipline, so that I can pass that on to Emily, and hopefully she'll turn out as good as me. . . . Just kidding!

MELISSA REEVES

$\mathcal{T}$he mother loves all her children—the stupid ones, the bright ones, the naughty ones, the good ones. It doesn't matter what their particular character is.

JOSEPH CAMPBELL

ABOUT MOTHERING

There's nothing more warm and sensitive than a child. You complete the full range of emotions. For me, that's what living is all about.

DONNA KARAN

I have never understood the fear of some parents about babies getting mixed up in the hospital. What difference does it make as long as you get a good one?

HEYWOOD BROUN

I think every working mom goes through the times when you feel that if you weren't working perhaps you'd be giving them a little more. I've always believed the quality of the time is so much more important than the quantity.

JACKIE ZEMAN

$\mathscr{A}$ baby is a mother's anchor. She cannot swing far from her moorings.

HENRY WARD BEECHER

$\mathscr{W}$hen motherhood becomes the fruit of a deep yearning, not the result of ignorance or accident, its children will become the foundation of a new race.

MARGARET SANGER

$\mathscr{W}$hen I was giving birth, the nurse asked, "Still think blondes have more fun?"

JOAN RIVERS

*I*n this day and age women can have kids for other women through surrogate motherhood. Is this the ultimate favor or what? I think I'm a good friend. I'll help you move. Okay. But whatever comes out of me after nine months, I'm keeping. I don't care if it's a shoe.

SUE KOLINSKY

*D*eath and taxes and childbirth! There's never any convenient time for any of them.

MARGARET MITCHELL

*C*hildbirth of course is not the grand finale but one point, albeit a very dramatic one, in the process of becoming a mother.

SHEILA KITZINGER

*M*otherhood was a scary, unknown thing, and work was familiar and secure. Work gave me more esteem as a mom. I thought, Okay, I can handle my job. Surely I can handle being this precious little girl's mom.

LEEZA GIBBONS

*I*f you bungle raising your children, I don't think whatever else you do well matters very much.

JACQUELINE KENNEDY ONASSIS

I hold her, knowing that she is terrified of my body and I am torn and terrified from her body and the agony and power of motherhood now is clear to me.

ROSEANNE

*Y*ou find out every woman, every pregnancy, every little baby's so unique. It was an experience I will never forget. A gift from God, that's the only thing you can say.

KATHIE LEE GIFFORD

I stood in the hospital corridor the night after she was born. Through a window I could see all the small, crying newborn infants and somewhere among them slept the one who was mine. I stood there for hours filled with happiness until the night nurse sent me to bed.

LIV ULLMANN

*T*he old-time mother who used to wonder where her boy was now has a grandson who wonders where his mother is.

KIN HUBBARD

I am *me*. I breast-feed my baby, and, yes, I do love to sew, and I do love to do all this fix-it stuff, but I still like interviewing the Secretary of State when given the chance. And if that makes me weird and different, sue me!

DEBORAH NORVILLE

A baby really changes you. Everything I thought was so important before is really just silliness.

DEIDRE HALL

That's what my children do for me—they give me stability and the sense of being complete.

LISA MARIE PRESLEY

I feel very blessed. There are so many women who have to go to work right away and have to leave their child, and I get to go to work and watch my daughter grow up. It's a tribute to the people I work with.

GABRIELLE CARTERIS

$\mathscr{A}$ mother should give her children a superabundance of enthusiasm, that after they have lost all they are sure to lose on mixing with the world, enough may still remain to prompt and support them through great actions.

JULIUS C. HARE

$\mathscr{I}$t sometimes happens, even in the best of families, that a baby is born. This is not necessarily cause for alarm. The important thing is to keep your wits about you and borrow some money.

ELINOR GOULDING SMITH

$\mathscr{A}$ccording to my method of thinking, and that of many others, not woman but the mother is the most precious possession of the nation, so precious that society advances its highest wellbeing when it protects the functions of the mother.

ELLEN KEY

$\mathcal{I}$'m going to protect this little life with everything I possibly can.

ANN JILLIAN

$\mathcal{G}$od knows that a mother needs fortitude and courage and tolerance and flexibility and patience and firmness and nearly every other brave aspect of the human soul. But because I happen to be a parent of almost fiercely maternal nature, I praise casualness. It seems to me the rarest of virtues. It is useful enough when children are small. It is important to the point of necessity when they are adolescents.

PHYLLIS McGINLEY

$\mathcal{M}$y role will be, above all, to make [this child] happy in what he does. Our children will not be unhappy.

PRINCESS STEPHANIE OF MONACO

$\mathcal{B}$eing a mom really puts a glint in your eye.

RACHEL HUNTER

*T*he most important thing a mother can do to promote her child's future welfare is modeling a happy, fulfilled person—somebody who is taking care of her own needs, who's happy, who's playful, who's creative.

LOIS GOBRECHT

*T*here's a depth linked to Sophie and the passion I have for her. I wouldn't have known about that without having had a child.

BETTE MIDLER

*M*oms are moms and they'll always want to share every little moment.

LYNN HERRING

I think we're seeing in working mothers a change from "Thank God it's Friday" to "Thank God it's Monday." If any working mother has not experienced that feeling, her children are not adolescent.

ANN DIEHL

*I*f I hadn't had a child, I'd never have known that most elemental, direct, true relationship. I don't know if I'd fully understand the values of society that I prize. I would have missed some of the mystery of life and death. Not to know how a child grows, the wonder of a newborn's hand . . . I have been fortunate.

DIANNE FEINSTEIN

*T*here's more to mothering than having kids, just as there's more to being an artist than owning a paintbrush.

HOLLY NORTH

I never thought that you should be rewarded for the greatest privilege of life.

MAY ROPER COKER,
ON BEING CHOSEN MOTHER OF THE YEAR

*O*ne of my children wrote in a third-grade piece on how her mother spent her time. . . . "one-half time on home, one-half time on outside things, one-half time writing."

CHARLOTTE MONTGOMERY

I knew having a baby would teach me about deep feelings of love, but I didn't know it would teach me so much about sharing.

DEIDRE HALL

*W*hat greater aspiration and challenge are there for a mother than the hope of raising a great son or daughter? [Motherhood is] a profession that was fully as interesting and challenging as any honorable profession.

ROSE KENNEDY

I just can't imagine life without my daughters. The littlest thing is a monumental experience.

JACKIE ZEMAN

$\mathcal{T}$he relationship between a mother and her children is almost telepathic. They feel what I feel and vice versa. It's the only relationship in the world that works that way. This doesn't happen between men and women. . . . I know because I've tried.

KATE MULGREW

$\mathcal{M}$y mother was always introducing me to young men who she thought were appropriate for me and whom I'd like, and I always resented that situation. But I find that I'm doing the same thing to my daughter.

CARMEN DUNCAN

$\mathcal{S}$omewhere down the line, when my children are grown, it would be interesting to get their perspective. I was concerned about it more when they were very little because I didn't know how it would turn out, but both my children are fabulous. As a mother, you try to guide your children and try to give them the benefit of your experience.

SUSAN LUCCI

*I*t is simply wonderful to have children, whether they are little toddlers or grown women and men on their own. When they are teen-agers, however, sometimes you wish you could cancel the whole deal.

NICKI MUTTER

I like being a Mom. I can dictate, not take dictation. I can call a baby sitter and take personal leave any time I want. And the boss is only three feet tall!

ESTHER PRESSER

*S*poil your husband, but don't spoil your children—that's my philosophy.

LOUISE S. G. CURREY
MOTHER OF THE YEAR

I think motherhood should be considered a profession, and it really *is* the oldest profession in the world.

NICOLE BEALE

Acknowledgments

Page 5. Mary Cassatt, *Reine Lefebvre Holding a Nude Baby*, (1902). Oil on canvas. Worcester Art Museum, Worcester, Massachusetts.

Page 11. Mary Cassatt, *Hélène de Septeuil*, (1889). Pastel on beige paper. The William Benton Museum of Art, The University of Connecticut. Louise Crombie Beach Memorial Collection.

Page 17. Mary Cassatt, *Young Mother Sewing*, (ca. 1900). Oil on canvas. The Metropolitan Museum of Art, Bequest of Mrs. H. O. Havemeyer, 1929. The H. O. Havemeyer Collection. (29.100.48)

Page 21. Mary Cassatt, *Mother and Child*, (1889). Oil on canvas. The Roland P. Murdock Collection, Wichita Art Museum, Wichita, Kansas.

Page 25. Mary Cassatt, *Children Playing on the Beach*, (1884). Oil on canvas. Ailsa Mellon Bruce Collection, © 1993 National Gallery of Art, Washington, D.C.

Page 31. Auguste Renoir, *Child with Toys - Gabrielle and the Artist's Son, Jean*, (ca. 1894), Oil on canvas. Collection of Mr. and Mrs. Paul Mellon, © 1993 National Gallery of Art, Washington, D.C.

Page 37. Mary Cassatt, *Women Admiring a Child*, (1897). Pastel on paper. © The Detroit Institute of Arts, Gift of Edward Chandler Walker.

Page 43. Mary Cassatt, American, 1844-1926, *The Bath*, Oil on canvas, 1891/92, 39-1/2 x 26 in., Robert A. Waller Fund, 1910.2. Photograph © 1993 The Art Institute of Chicago. All Rights Reserved.

Page 49. *After the Bath*. Pastel, ca. 1901, 64.8 x 99.7 cm. Mary Cassatt, American, 1845-1926. © The Cleveland Museum of Art, Gift of J. H. Wade, 20.379.